GW00721750

HEROES OF THE WILD WEST

ANNIE OAKLEY

BY
Penny Stempel

This edition first published by Parragon Books in 1995

Produced by
Magpie Books Ltd, London

Copyright © Parragon Book Service Ltd 1995
Unit 13–17, Avonbridge Trading Estate
Atlantic Road
Avonmouth
Bristol BS11 9QD

Cover picture and illustrations courtesy of
Peter Newark's Western Americana

ISBN 0-75250-775-3

A copy of the British Library Cataloguing in Publication
Data is available from the British Library.

Typeset by Hewer Text Composition Services, Edinburgh
Printed in Singapore by Printlink International Co.

HEROES OF THE WILD WEST
Annie Oakley

Childhood

No more unlikely background for a Wild West markswoman could be imagined than that of Annie Oakley. Her parents, Jacob and Susan Moses, were devout Quakers whose home was almost chapel-like in its religious tranquility. She wasn't even a westerner. Yet from these improbable beginnings emerged one of the world's best-known, and best-loved, entertainers.

Legend tells how a mature Jacob fell in love with fifteen-year-old Susan Wise, placed her on a pillion and carried her away on his horse. They married in Blair County, Pennsylvania, in 1850 and became the parents of Mary Jane, Lyda and Elizabeth. To earn their keep, the couple kept a small inn on the Pennsylvania Canal. One night, when a careless guest tipped an oil-lamp onto the sawdust floor, the log tavern caught fire and burned to the ground, leaving the family homeless. It was 1855. Jacob had heard tell of the fertile Ohio country, and he and Susan packed up their few possessions and moved west to the promise of a new life. To aid his survival on the unruly frontier, Jacob took with him his trusty muzzle-loader. It was this gun that was to shoot young Phoebe Ann Moses into a career that was the stuff of myth and history.

Darke County, Ohio, is farmland hewn from thick, virgin forest. After General Anthony Wayne built his fort at Greenville and defeated the Indians at the Battle of Fallen Timbers, White settlers flocked in to clear the forests and plant corn and graze cows. Jacob and Susan Moses settled in northern Darke County, just outside the small village of Woodland and not far from the county town of Greenville. Here Jacob built a cabin of rough timbers, and five more children were born: Sarah Ellen, Phoebe Ann, on 13

August 1860, John, Hulda and a daughter who died in infancy. Phoebe Ann grew into a small child, strong for her size, with thick dark hair and large, bright blue-grey eyes. Nick-named 'Annie' by her sisters, she spurned their rag dolls, preferring instead to play with her father and her younger brother John.

Young Annie's first memories were of roaming the Darke County woods near by. She tracked rabbits, and collected hickory nuts, red haws, wal-nuts and wild cherries. With her three older sisters, she hunted fox-grapes in the woods and crayfish in the creek; she took pleasure in the roses, the birds and the wild ducks and geese which flew free. By the age of seven she was trapping quail and rabbit for the family table. At the age of eight she fired her first gun, and this legendary first shot was to change the course of her life for ever.

Jacob Moses had hung his old Kentucky rifle over the fireplace in the family cabin. One day Annie saw a squirrel run over the grass in front of the house, through an orchard and onto a fence where it paused to get a hickory nut. She ran into the house, fetched a chair and collected the gun. Once outside, she rested the barrel on the porch railing and took aim. The shot went straight through the squirrel's head, from side to side. Annie was to tell the tale for the rest of her years. 'I was eight years old when I took my first shot,' she would say, 'and I still consider it one of the best shots I ever made.'

Annie's carefree early childhood ended abruptly on a snowy day in 1866. Jacob Moses had set out to take his corn and wheat to the local market fourteen miles away, and while he was gone a blizzard set in. At midnight, Susan Moses and her young children were still staring out anxiously at the furious snow when the wagon came, a blurred grey shape in the swirl of white, a ghostly figure huddled on the seat. Annie's father sat upright in the buckboard seat, his hands frozen and his speech gone. The doctor came, but there was little he could do. Annie's father died that March.

The destitute family moved to a rented farm, but matters did not improve. Annie's oldest sister, Mary Jane, died of tuberculosis, and Susan Moses was so poor that she had her youngest child Hulda adopted. Phoebe Ann fared no better. In 1870, when Annie was ten years old, Mrs Crawford Edington, matron at Darke County Infirmary, Greenville, offered to take the young girl and train her in exchange for help with the institution's children. The infirmary was the dumping ground for the elderly, the orphaned and the insane, but so desperate was Susan

Moses that she could not refuse.

This early experience was to leave Annie with an abiding compassion for children, manifested wherever she went. It also taught her a skill and appreciation for fine sewing, which proved invaluable when she later designed and crafted her famous, fine-fitting costumes. The Edingtons paid her to work as a seamstress, and she sewed dresses and made quilts for the home's inmates. She learned to embroider and stitched fancy cuffs and collars to brighten the orphans' dark dresses.

She was fifteen when she went back to live with her mother, who had mar-

ried Joseph Shaw and was living in a
cabin at North Star, not far from
Woodland. Annie's love of shooting
together with her stepfather's round as
a mail-carrier were to bring her a new
livelihood – and to carry her one step
closer to her sharpshooting destiny.

Butler and Oakley

The Katzenberger brothers' grocery store in Greenville lay on the corner of Main Street and the public square, and hunters and trappers could trade in their wild turkeys and rabbits there. Joseph Shaw regularly made two trips a week carrying mail to Greenville – now on each trip he carried Annie's grouse, quail and rabbits and exchanged them for ammunition, groceries and necessities. G. Anthony and Charles Katzenberger shipped Annie's game on to hotels in Cincinnati and Dayton, and to the famous Golden Lamb in Lebanon. As time went on, the good brothers could not get enough of Annie's game. Hotel-keepers would request it, and the diners at Bevis House in Cincinnati commented to the manager Jack Frost on its quality. Annie was so good, she shot every animal through the head. That way, there was never any in the shot meat.

Annie Moses became a familiar sight around North Star, a slim girl of sixteen dressed in a short, sturdy dress with knickerbockers and heavy mittens with a trigger-finger stitched in.

Annie Oakley.

Covered Wagons, N.C. Wyeth.

She knew the habits of quail and the feeding-places of grouse. She trapped rabbits in binder twine and caught quail in cornstalk traps covered by brush and baited with grains of corn. At first, she took aim with Jacob Moses's old long-barrelled cap-and-ball Pennsylvania rifle; later, she shot with a Parker Brothers 16-gauge breech-loading hammer.

While Annie sharpened her eye in the woods of Darke County, 'champion marksmen' Baughman and Butler were one of many popular acts touring variety theatres with a fancy shooting display. Irish immigrant Frank Butler was a trim young man with dark hair and a small moustache. He had learned trick shooting and could delight an audience by sighting through a mirror or firing a rifle while bending over backwards. The two men were joined in their act by Frank's pet poodle, George.

In the spring of 1881, Baughman and Butler had teamed up with the re-nowned Sells Brothers Circus – 'the Biggest Amusement Enterprise on Earth' – to perform in Cincinnati. Under the wing of the brothers Ephraim, Lewis, Peter and Allen, the two marksmen became 'the Champion Rifle Dead-Shots of the World'. Circus couriers trumpeted the duo's 'unri-valled off-hand, snap-shot, bull's-eye programme of startling, dexterous, critical hits'. Baughman and Butler shattered glass balls, aimed backwards while sighting in a mirror, and shot apples off each other's head at fifteen paces.

By chance, while playing in Cincinnati, the two men were staying under the roof of hotel-keeper Jack Frost, avid customer of Annie Moses's shot-free game. As the performers boasted of their peerless skills, Frost had an idea: he would match the youthful huntress in a shooting contest with Butler. He told Frank he had an unknown who would shoot against him at Greenville ten days from that time for $100 a side. 'It seemed a shame for me to take the money from those country people,'

Frank later said. But he needed the money, and he went. Both the match and the marriage that followed were to be immortalized on the silver screen.

Frank Butler arrived in Greenville on a late spring day to find the county out in force in defence of their 'unknown'. He was later to tell eager reporters the tale. How did he feel when he discovered that his opponent was none other than little Annie Moses? 'I almost dropped dead when a little slim girl in short dresses stepped out to the mark with me,' he recalled. And what of the legendary match itself? 'I was a beaten man the moment she appeared for I was taken off guard,' he declared. 'Never were the birds so hard for two shooters as they flew from us, but never did a person make more impossible shots than did that little girl. She killed 23 and I killed 21. It was her first big match — my first defeat.'

He was not only a beaten man, he was a man in love; with one failed marriage behind him, he had fallen for the young sharpshooter in linsey dress and knickerbockers. He invited Annie to a theatre to see his act. She went, and watched as Frank shot an apple from the head of his poodle, George. George picked up a piece of apple and laid it at Annie's feet, and when Frank left to join the circus he sent greetings to Annie via George. When Christmas came, the faithful pooch sent Annie candy, letters, and a poem written by Frank.

> 'There's a charming little girl
> She's many miles from here
> She's a loving little fairy
> You'd fall in love to see her
> Her presence would remind you
> Of an angel in the skies,
> And you bet I love this little girl
> With the rain drops in her eyes.'

Annie Moses was twenty years old, but worldly-wise Frank Butler was her first suitor. Around a year after their first meeting – 20 June 1882 – he became her husband. By 1883, Annie and Frank were partners on stage, and the shooting team of Butler and Oakley was born.

Annie had joined her husband on tour with his new act, Graham and Butler, 'America's Own Rifle Team and Champion All-Round Shots'. John Graham and Butler wore tall black boots, tight trousers, and coats with tails. Frank fired bending over backwards, John with his rifle upside down between his legs. They were a hit with audiences wherever they went – until John Graham fell ill. Frank asked Annie to join him as his stage-assistant, holding up objects to serve as his targets. One night, Frank missed his target a dozen times, and a rowdy crowd called out for the girl to have a shot. Annie had never before attempted the shot, but on the second try she hit the target. The crowd went into uproar, Frank was howled down and Annie continued. From that day on, although Frank's name was to the fore, it was Annie who was the main attraction. Frank taught her all he knew, and then willingly stepped aside. 'She outclassed me,' he gallantly explained.

Annie Oakley outclassed them all. Dressed simply in a dark dress with a starched white collar and pretty cuffs at the sleeve, she stood only five feet tall and weighed about 110 pounds. Her thick dark hair was cut close round her face and hung long over her shoulders, and her winning smile and dainty performance held a rare magnetism for all who watched.

A pioneer family outside their timber cabin.

An idealized view of the West, from a lithograph of 1868.

The name – Annie Oakley – Annie Moses conjured up herself. Some say she took it after a visit to Oakley, Cincinna; others, that it was an old family name. Either way, from 1882 Annie Oakley was her name, and that was how she was known to the world and to herself from then on.

Annie Oakley's early days on stage gave no hint of the fame and fortune to come. Travelling by train, on the cheapest possible fare, Butler and Oakley travelled the Midwest – Ohio, Michigan, Indiana, Wisconsin, Illinois – rooming in drab boarding-houses, changing costumes in drafty dressing-rooms, coming on stage after the jugglers and before the dog and pony show. Frank had nothing to teach Annie – she knew it all. In her pleated skirt and crisp embroidered jacket, she shot coins out of a man's hand and cards from the air. The only hard part was the stage lighting: at best, flames which sputtered and sparked; at worst, non-existent. Frank took a back seat. He placed the ads, made the bookings and consulted the train time-tables. 'I owe whatever I have', Annie would say, 'to my husband's careful management.'

But the pair tired of their hand-to-mouth existence, and signed a forty-week contract with the Sells Brothers Circus, due to start in April 1884. Annie was to join Mr Orrin Hollins, world-vanquishing Spanish equestrian, Prince Fokio, the Japanese juggling marvel, fifty double-somersault leapers and the world's only performing hippopotamus. Far from claiming a starring role, Annie doubled as Mrs Old One-Two in a pantomime while Frank played Quaker Starchback. Butler and Oakley's last independent engagement was in March of that year at the Olympic Theater, St Paul, Minnesota. It was there that Annie Oakley met *Tatanka Iyotake* – Chief Sitting Bull.

Sitting Bull was blamed for the 'murder' of General George Armstrong Custer in the summer of 1876 at the Little Bighorn. Dakota Territory's most distinguished political prisoner, Sitting Bull was allowed to leave the Standing Rock Agency at Fort Yates so long as permission was granted by James McLaughlin, Indian agent at the fort. One of the great Sioux chief's trips was to St Paul, where his tour of the city took in a night at the theatre. Sitting Bull had seen much in his time, but he was unprepared for the rifle tricks of the nimble, diminutive Annie Oakley with the flowing dark hair. As Annie ran out of the ring, Sitting Bull followed. At the door of her tent, his deep voice boomed out the words 'Wantanyeya Ciscila' – 'Little Sure-shot'. The great chief had adopted the charismatic young markswoman as chieftain's daughter, an honour

which carried with it the right, should
she wish to take up residence in Indian
country, to receive five ponies, a
wigwam, cattle and other livestock.
Annie declined Sitting Bull's offer,
but was quick to take up another –
the chance to star in the Buffalo Bill
Wild West Show.

Buffalo Bill's Wild West Show

It was in New Orleans, December 1884. The Sells Brothers Circus season had come to an end and Butler and Oakley were without when a job William F. Cody, better known as Buffalo Bill, rode into town. Buffalo Bill wore buckskin shirt and leggings, and bristled with revolvers, knives and rifles. Tall, handsome, and strong, with long black hair and a

The young Annie supplied game
to local hotels.

Frank Butler.

goatee beard, from the age of fourteen he had worked the western
plains as a scout and Indian-fighter.
His name was earned when he killed
4,280 buffalo in eight months to feed
the twelve hundred-strong crew of
the Kansas Pacific Railroad. His
authentic Wild West Show boasted
cowboys on bucking broncos, Indians beating tom-toms, stagecoach
ambushes, buffalo, elk and world-
famous fancy shooter Captain Bogardus. When the good Captain quit the
show, Annie saw her opportunity. A
quickly penned note to Colonel
Cody brought an invitation to a
three-day trial, and by the end of
April 1885 Annie Oakley joined the
show.

But Cody had doubted that Annie's stamina was equal to the strenuous fancy-shooting act required. Nothing if not proud, Annie determined to prove herself. Armed with three 16-gauge Parker shotguns, she attempted to break 5,000 glass balls in one day – a feat which would make her the equal of any sharpshooter and prove her as able as the great Captain Bogardus himself. After nine hours she had broken 4,772 balls. She was ready for Buffalo Bill.

If Annie was unknown when she joined the Wild West Show, 'Annie Oakley, the peerless wing and rifle shot' soon had solo billing. She was to stay with Buffalo Bill's outfit for

seventeen years. Her act was short but
skilful; her presence on stage, mag-
netic. As the white canvas curtains
parted, Little Sureshot tripped in,
waving, bowing and blowing kisses.
Flowers were embroidered on her tan,
pleated skirt and ribbons stitched along
its hem just below her knees – the
hard-learned lessons in Darke County
Infirmary had stood her in good stead.
A six-pointed star was pinned to her
sombrero, and from her knees to her
shoes she wore laced, pearl-buttoned
leggings which she cut and fitted to
perfection herself.

Her act took place in the centre of the
arena where her rifles and shotguns lay
ready under a silk drape on a plain

wooden table. Frank released clay
birds for her singly, then in pairs, then
triplets and finally four at a time. Her
speed and accuracy were a sight to
behold. Her skill was such that she
could shoot the centre-spot out of a
five of spades dropped from a flag-
pole. Whether she shot with her left
hand or her right, with the rifle upside
down over her head or while she was
lying on her back across a chair, she
never failed to shatter the glass balls.
She broke balls twirled by Frank on
the end of a rope; she threw two balls
in the air, grabbed her gun, and hit
both before they touched the ground;
and she could turn her back on her
target and aim over her shoulder by
sighting in a small mirror or even a

shiny table-knife. One newspaper cal-
culated that she could turn, sight, and
hit a falling target in no more than half
a second.

Annie most dazzling act took a mere
ten seconds and, show-woman that
she was, she kept it until last. First
she laid five shotguns on her table.
Then she took her rifle in her hands
and held it upside down. At her signal,
Frank threw the glass balls into the air,
one after another. She smashed the first
with her inverted rifle, and then
picked up each shotgun in turn, dis-
charged both barrels and shattered two
more balls. She exchanged guns five
times and broke eleven glass balls in
less than a second each. As she laid the

last smoking gun on the table, she blew
a kiss to the audience and disappeared
behind the curtains, pausing only for
the briefest of moments as she exited to
give her humorous little trade-mark
kick.

Annie soon proved to be a huge
attraction, in no small part because of
her rare ability to work a crowd.
Before a difficult shot she would stand
and concentrate, hand on hips. If she
missed, she would stamp her foot; if
she succeeded, she gave a kick of
delight. 'When she doesn't hit a ball,
she pouts,' the *New York Sun* told its
readers. 'She evidently thinks a good
deal of her pout, because she turns to
the audience to show it off.' Before

long, her name would be on the lips of every man, woman and child in America and Europe.

It was in 1886 that Little Sureshot conquered New York. Erastus Wiman, president of the Staten Island Amusement Company, had built a fifty-acre open-air arena (illuminated for night-trim performances with new electric arc-lights) on Staten Island, and Buffalo Bill's Wild West Show was to play there for the summer. 'Erastina Woods' was only a short ride from Manhattan, and, to aid visitors, a fleet of ferryboats had been chartered and four miles of narrow-gauge railway built to run from Mariners Harbor to the Erastina gateway.

They were ready for the crowds, and the crowds came. 'Staten Island Trembles Beneath the Tread of Painted Warriors on the War-Path' declared the newspapers. 'Just Like Real Fighting, Indians Fall From Horses and Look Like Dead Men.' Twenty thousand people filled the stands.

By now, Annie Oakley travelled in some comfort. Her tent was filled with knick-knacks and portraits, satin pillows and buckskin trappings, all arranged in an artistic fashion. The floor was even covered with Axminster carpet. For this season, however, Annie also had competition in the Wild West Show. It came in the shape of fifteen-year-old Miss Lillian

Frances Smith, 'The California Huntress and Champion Girl Rifle Shot'. It was no doubt because of Miss Smith's arrival that Annie Oakley was so determined not to miss the great New York opening parade.

At daybreak on 26 June, Annie was in an agony of pain. During the show's last Washington performance, in the middle of her act, a furious buzzing had filled her right ear. She finished her act to the crowd's applause, but the pain pierced deeper. Unbeknown to her, an insect had lodged near her eardrum, and now, despite all Frank's ministrations, she was running a high fever. The parade was to have Indians in paint and feathers, Mexicans in their brightest serapes, and cowboys combing out their mustangs' manes. But the doctor told Annie she must lie quietly for at least three days.

It was the only parade of the summer and the longest they would ever make. Annie had sewn a new costume for it with everything matching, right down to the cloth trappings for her horse with 'Oakley' stitched on either side. 'That parade in New York meant everything to me,' Annie was later to relate. A mere fever was not going to stop the girl who had come so far from Darke County, and she called to a groom to saddle her horse. With Buffalo Bill at its head, the procession crossed Twenty-third Street to Eighth

Annie Oakley in her distinctive pleated skirt
and decorative jacket.

Poster for one of Annie Oakley's rivals.

Avenue, went up Eighth Avenue to
Forty-second, across Forty-second
Street to Fifth Avenue, down Fifth
Avenue and Broadway to the Bat-
tery. The street was filled with people, the band played, and horses
stamped and whinnied. Sitting side-
saddle, Annie Oakley rode for three
hours in the hot June sun, waving to
the thousands massed under the trees
of Madison Square. When it was time
to dismount, Annie was too weak
even to slide down from her pony.
She had to be carried to her tent. The
next morning, the doctor came.
'Blood poisoning,' he declared.

Annie Oakley was so weak she was
unable to sit up, and every afternoon

that week the show went on without her. For four days she tossed and turned in her tent. On the fifth day, though her face was still swollen, she insisted she must perform. With her hat hiding a white bandage, so weak that she had to lean against her gun-table as she aimed, she put out six candles on a turning wheel in six quick shots. She had missed four shows – the only performances she would miss in seventeen years and 170,000 miles of travel.

Europe

A regular visitor to Staten Island that summer was Mark Twain, himself no stranger to the prairies, the swaying stagecoach and the Indian camps. After his second visit, he wrote Buffalo Bill an enthusiastic letter:

'Dear Mr Cody,
I have now seen your Wild West Show two days in succession, and

have enjoyed it thoroughly. It brought vividly back the breezy wild life of the plains and the Rocky Mountains. Down to its smallest details the Show is genuine – cowboys, vaqueros, Indians, stagecoach, costumes and all; it is wholly free from sham and insincerity and the effects it produced upon me by its spectacles were identical with those wrought upon me a long time ago on the frontier. Your pony expressman was as tremendous an interest to me yesterday as he was twenty-three years ago when he used to come whizzing by from over the desert with his war news; and your bucking horses

Annie Oakley shows off her target skills.

Buffalo Bill Cody.

were even painfully real to me as
I rode one of those outrages once
for nearly a quarter of a minute. It
is often said on the other side of
the water that none of the exhibitions which we send to England are purely and distinctively
American. If you will take the
Wild West Show over there you
can remove that reproach.

Yours truly,
MARK TWAIN

And indeed, just as the eminent Mark
Twain had suggested, one year later
Buffalo Bill's Wild West Show set sail
for London on the steamship *State of
Nebraska*. In England's capital, Annie

Oakley was to win an introduction to Queen Victoria herself.

Scores of people gathered at the foot of Leroy Street to wave farewell to Buffalo Bill and his entourage. The scene on board the huge new steamship loaded with its unfamiliar cargo was, according to the *New York Times*, 'as gay as a ballet'. Horses, mules, steers and buffalo were all on board thanks to cowboys swinging the knotted ends of lariats, whooping and jabbing. When animals and scenery, wagons, saddles and the battered Deadwood stage-coach were all loaded, Red Shirt, Little Bull, Cut Meat and Poor Dog filed aboard, fearful of what lay in store. Legend said that any Indian who crossed the big water would waste away and die. As the gangway swung aboard and the engines sprang into life deep in the ship, a cowboy band on the promenade played 'The Girl I Left Behind Me'. Eleven days later, the *State of Nebraska* arrived at the shore of England. As they docked they were met by swarms of London newsmen, who imparted to their readers excited accounts of 'moccasins, feathers, beads, and warpaint'. The Wild West had come to the Old World.

London had been well prepared for the show at Earl's Court. Posters everywhere announced Buffalo Bill's arrival, and Annie Oakley, in her doeskin skirt and beaded jacket, was recognized wherever she walked. A reporter from The *Globe* made this comment in rhyme on the ubiquitous placards:

'I may walk it or bus it, or
   hansom cab it; still
I am faced by the features of
   Buffalo Bill;
Every hoarding is plastered,
   from East End to West
With his hat, coat and countenance,
   lovelocks and vest.'

Earl's Court covered twenty-three acres of gardens, courts and exhibition halls. That year, it was to be home to a trade fair called the American Exhibition, and the Wild West Show was to play alongside it. An arena was prepared for the show, with seating for thirty thousand around an oval a third of a mile long. At the end of the horseshoe was a huge backdrop showing a panorama of plains and rugged mountains.

It was not the American Exhibition, featuring the best and newest of all American goods, which excited exposition-weary Londoners. It was the Wild West camp to which visitors came in throngs, many of them prestigious. On 28 April, the Prime Minister and his wife called at the camp. Mr Gladstone smoked a cigar with Cody, and Mrs Gladstone chatted with Annie Oakley in her dressing-tent.

Royalty was equally anxious to catch the show which was the talk of the town. On 6 May, Edward, the Prince of Wales, observed with pleasure from his royal box as Buffalo Bill staged an impromptu command–performance prior to the show's opening. Three days later, a liveried messenger brought word that Queen Victoria, who was celebrating her jubilee after fifty years on the throne, requested a performance for herself and her jubilee guests. On the appointed morning, the Queen arrived in her royal carriage, while other carriages brought the King of Denmark, the King and Queen of Belgium, the King of Saxony, the King of Greece, the Crown Prince of Austria, the Crown Prince of

Sitting Bull wearing a hat given to him by
'Little Sureshot'.

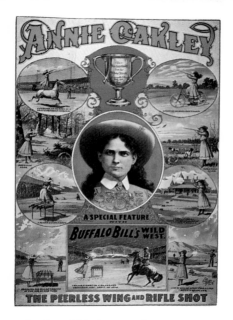

Annie quickly became the star of the
Wild West Show.

Germany, Grand Duke Michael of Russia, Prince Louis of Baden and assorted dukes, duchesses, lords and ladies.

Annie Oakley opened the show, galloping into the empty arena, leaning from the saddle, snatching a pistol from the ground and shattering a series of flying targets. With her final shot, a herd of buffalo appeared, and Indians swept across the floor with cries and gunfire; then cowboys thundered past, racing the stampede past the royal stand.

Once again, there was a presentation for the Wild West Show performers. As Annie was introduced to the black-bonneted monarch, Queen Victoria smiled at her. 'You are a very clever little girl,' she said.

Annie Oakley's tent was filled with gifts and flowers, and every mail brought hundreds of admiring letters. She showed her trunk of guns and pistols, her badges and medals and her gifts from Sitting Bull, to thousands of visitors. She entertained newspaper reporters with American juices and refreshments and they in turn wrote of the marvellous shootist who was only twenty years old. (She was now in fact twenty-seven, but to her adoring public she was, and would always remain a mere girl of twenty).

London seemed more interested in
Annie Oakley than in Buffalo Bill
himself. One summer morning, a
note arrived for Colonel Cody:
Would Miss Annie Oakley shoot a
friendly match with Grand Duke
Michael of Russia? Annie Oakley
willingly agreed, and two days later
four carriages brought princes and
princesses to the royal box to watch
the match. The Grand Duke fancied
himself as a sportsman, but the girl
from the American prairies defeated
the Russian Grand Duke: each of
them shot fifty birds, but Annie
scored 47 to the Grand Duke's 36.

By the end of the summer, two and a
half million people had visited the

Wild West Show at Earl's Court. It was Annie Oakley who had drawn the longest applause in the arena and the most attention in the papers. On 3 October, the gates were closed. As Annie Oakley left London, a new book was on show in all the shop-windows. *The Rifle Queen*, published by the General Publishing Co., recounted the 'truthful and stirring story' of Annie Oakley in sixty-four drama-packed pages. Annie Oakley was already a legend.

When the Wild West Show train pulled out of West Brompton station, Annie Oakley was not aboard. She had a more important appointment – with Kaiser Wilhelm of

Germany. Crown Prince Wilhelm had asked Annie Oakley to shoot for the Emperor at Charlottenburg Palace. Annie and Frank travelled by train to Berlin, and were driven in the imperial carriage to the famous Charlottenburg Racecourse on the curving River Spree. The Emperor was indisposed that day, but Prince Wilhelm watched as Annie Oakley, all alone in the empty arena, shot first a line of clay pigeons, then a run of live pigeons, and pulverized pairs of coloured balls, one after another.

After the show, Prince Wilhelm strode across the grass. As Annie curtsied he asked her if she would repeat a trick he had seen her perform in London:

would she extinguish with her gun a
lighted cigarette held between his lips?
He lit a cigarette and held it in his
mouth as Annie paced away. She
turned, raised her gun and fired; the
cigarette stopped smoking. The little
girl from Darke County had conquered another European capital with
her dazzling fancy shooting feats.

Paris was next to fall captive to her
charms. 1889 was the year of the
Exposition Universel and the erection of
one of the wonders of the world – the
Eiffel Tower. It was also the year in
which thirty acres of fashionable Paris
became the American frontier. At the
edge of the Bois de Bologne, just a short
distance from the Arc de Triomphe,

Broadway, New York, in the 1880s.

Annie Oakley was badly injured in a train crash in 1901.

Indians had their camp, the mountains of Montana rose high and steers and buffalo were corralled. On the opening day of the Wild West Show, 18 May, twenty thousand people filled the stands to see Annie Oakley shoot the flames off a revolving wheel of candles and shoot two pairs of twin targets, each pair with a different gun. Her greatest triumph that season was a new pistol stunt with playing-cards putting a bullet through the ace of hearts. Annie pierced the ace of hearts head-on from twenty paces, then she turned the playing card sideways and split it down the edge with a bullet. Over the next few years she was to become renowned for her feats with cards. If Frank Butler held out a visiting card edgeways to her at a distance of up to twenty paces, the newspapers reported incredulously, Annie Oakley could hit the hair-thin edge of the card with a bullet from a pistol.

By midsummer, Paris shopkeepers were unable to meet the demand for Indian blankets, bows and arrows, moccasins, buffalo robes, bearskins, lariats and high-horned Western saddles. Annie Oakley was presented at receptions and garden parties, made an honorary member of gun clubs and riding clubs, and awarded an honorary commission in the French Army by President Carnot.

There followed three years in which cities throughout Europe surrendered their hearts to the *petite* sharpshooter. Frank and Annie visited Marseilles, Lyons, Barcelona, Naples, Rome, Florence, Bologna, Pisa and Milan, Verona, Venice, Munich and Vienna. A second tour took in Stuttgart, Karlsruhe, Mannheim, Mainz, Wiesbaden, Cologne, Dortmund, Duisburg and Aachen. From Germany, the Wild West Show travelled through Belgium and Holland, and then crossed the North Sea into England for a long tour of the British Isles.

Home

Annie was thirty-one when she came home with the Wild West Show aboard the steamship *Mohawk*, which tied up at a wharf along the Hudson River on 27 October 1892. She returned to the United States a star, and she brought with her considerable savings amassed in the years of performing.

With their new-found wealth the

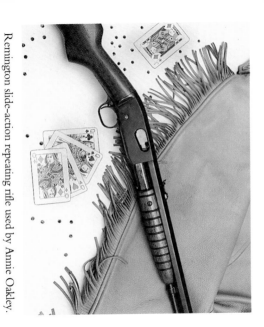

Remington slide-action repeating rifle used by Annie Oakley.

The world famous sharpshooter takes aim.

Butlers began searching New Jersey
for a house to buy. After a decade of
travel, they had a strong desire for a
settled home, and they chose the little
town of Nutley in which to nest. Only
thirteen miles from New York City,
Nutley was home to a number of
writers and artists who built their
studios overlooking the tree-lined
Passaic River which wound through
the town. There, Frank and Annie
bought a plot from Mr J. Fisher
Satterthwaite and began building the
house of their dreams late in 1892.
Shortly before Christmas 1893, they
moved into their new house at 304
Grant Avenue. A spacious house
which cost nine thousand dollars, it
had three storeys, a porch across the

front, a railed balcony and a turret. Legend has it that Annie had the house built entirely without closets because she was so used to living out of a trunk.

But if her domestic life had taken on a more peaceful pace, Annie's showmanship with the Wild West Show continued unabated. 1894 saw the show sited at Ambrose Park, South Brooklyn, which it transformed into a familiar city of coloured flags and flowers. The rodeodrama was even more thrilling now than it had been ten years before at Erastina, with the addition of soldiers of many nations. Adding to the glamour was an enormous electric-light system which enabled the show to play at night. The lights were so powerful that they could illumine boats in the harbour and were visible from beyond the Statue of Liberty.

That September, Buffalo Bill, his Indians and Annie Oakley were invited to appear before Thomas A. Edison's new battery-driven movie camera, the kinetograph, housed in a black-draped room which was the first ever motion-picture studio. Edison was particularly pleased with his record of Annie Oakley's performance because his machine proved sensitive enough to reproduce the smoke from her guns and the shattering of the breaking balls. The pictures that lived and moved for ninety seconds were shown in the kinetoscope parlours that opened in New

York in 1894, and crowds waited in long lines to catch a glimpse. Eventually, the movie industry spawned by Edison's kinetoscope would lead to the demise of the great Wild West shows whose stars had been its earliest subjects.

But the change in the Wild West Show's fortunes began long before that, at Ambrose Park. Gate receipts were low and, for the first time ever, were outstripped by the show's massive costs. Cody gave up his plans for a permanent base in South Brooklyn and took the Wild West Show on the road.

For the Wild West Show, 1901 was another wearying year travelling the country. There were just two show dates to go before the season ended: Monday, 28 October, in Charlotte, North Carolina, and Tuesday, 29 October, in Danville, Virginia. The stands were crowded that Monday night in Charlotte. Twelve thousand people passed through the gates and admired Annie's prodigious skills. No one could have guessed that this was to be Annie Oakley's last ever performance as a member of Buffalo Bill's Wild West Show.

They loaded the Show trains in Charlotte at midnight. It was a clear, crisp night. The stateroom was warm. As the train moved off, the lights of Charlotte dropped behind. Then there was nothing but darkness and the hum of the rails.

As Annie and Frank slept, just north of the little town of Linwood, the head-lamp of another train appeared on the single track ahead. A freight train was running south from Greensboro. The conductor should have waited on a siding for the show train to pass, but instead he gave full throttle. It was 2.30 a.m. The engines met head-on. There was a thunderous crash and the night air was filled with the sounds of rending iron and splintering wood. Five stock-cars shattered and fell into a ditch. Under the mass of wrecked timber and rolling-stock were trapped the groaning bodies of dying horses. Not one horse from the first five coaches of the train was saved – a hundred Wild West Show horses were crushed to death. No one was killed, but four railway employees were injured.

At home in Nutley the next day, Annie Oakley sat up in bed. When Frank brought her mirror, brush and comb, she stared in disbelief. Her beautiful long dark hair had turned white overnight. And not only her hair had changed. Extensive internal injuries had paralysed her left side. She spent months in hospital before returning home, and only then with a brace on her leg. It took all of Annie's patience and determination to shoot again.

Only one year after leaving Buffalo Bill, Annie was back on stage aiming her gun once more, but now she had a

new career – as an actress. At Atlantic
City, on 12 November 1902, the
curtain went up at Young's Pier
Theater on Langdon McCormick's
new melodrama, *The Western Girl*. It
was written especially for Annie, and
she gave it her all. She played Nancy
Barry, the good daughter of a bad
bandit, the girl who saved the life of
the young lieutenant and put the Silver
Creek bandits to rout. It was a play
made to order. Annie still wore her
short skirts, her leggings and her sombrero (with the addition of a curly
brown wig to cover her now white
hair). She shot a bottle out of her
drunken father's hand, blasted her
way out of a room where she was
kept prisoner, and smashed twenty

glass balls in a row. It was rousing stuff, and Annie saved the day.

When the troupe broke up, Annie went on tour with Frank. He was travelling the country as a representative for the Union Metallic Cartridge Company, promoting their products at one gun club after another. No better advertisement could have been found than Annie's sharpshooting skills, and soon she was giving free exhibitions for UMC wherever Frank went. In the summer of 1906 she performed in Dubois, Pennsylvania, and gave a show to match any in the Wild West Show itself. She broke small wooden balls thrown in the air, and then shattered the pieces before they reached the ground; she hit brass discs, pennies, and .22 cartridges; she shot the ashes off Frank's cigarette; she clipped four pieces of chalk that Frank held between his fingers; she rolled a tin can away from her with rapid shots; and she smashed eggs thrown in the air at a distance of fifty yards. 'It was the most remarkable exhibition ever witnessed in Dubois,' exclaimed the *Morning Journal*.

After a decade out of the spotlight, Annie Oakley itched to get on the road again. In 1911, she had a letter from the Young Buffalo show. The contract was generous, the coffers were low and the house in Nutley had been sold back in 1904. Annie and Frank packed the costumes and the guns, and hitched up. It was like old times back in the sawdust ring – horsemen and Indians, steers and buffalo, the roar of voices as Annie splintered targets in the arena. From Illinois they crossed the Midwest, travelled up into Canada and moved down the coast.

The Young Buffalo show took her to 139 towns in seventeen states. Then, in 1913, fifty-three-year-old Annie Oakley retired as a Wild West star. At Marion, Illinois, on 4 October 1913, Annie rode in her last street parade and gave her last fancy-shooting stage performance before settling down.

Final Years

Pinehurst, North Carolina, was a picturesque village of winding paths planted with flowers and shrubs. It had four hotels, a clubhouse, two golf-courses and a dozen stores. The Carolina was Pinehurst's finest hotel. It stood four storeys tall, had lifts, and had steam-heat, electric lights and telephones in every room. In 1915, Annie Oakley and Frank Butler took up residence at the Carolina Hotel. They earned their keep by teaching at the Pinehurst gun club: Frank worked at the skeets, Annie at the trap- and rifle-range. It was a life of guns, dogs, horses and relaxed, congenial people.

They were at Pinehurst in January 1917 when newspaper headlines brought them sad news: 'Buffalo Bill Dies in Denver'. He had died, all but forgotten, on a cold January morning. When America entered the war that year, the same newspapers recalled that Annie Oakley had once shot a cigarette out of the mouth of the Crown Prince of Germany, now Kaiser Wilhelm, and deplored that her aim had been so accurate. Now Annie was sent on a tour of American training-camps to give rifle demonstrations for the troops.

Season after season, Annie won matches and established records. In the spring of 1922, at Pinehurst, shooting from sixteen yards, she broke a hundred clay targets in succession. There were rumours of a come-back in October 1922, when she made a triumphant appearance at the forty-ninth Brockton fair in Massachusetts. But fate was to intervene.

As the November winds brought chill thoughts of snow, Annie and Frank decided to spend the winter season with friends in Florida. One week after arriving, on Thursday, 9 November, they were driving with their friends along the Dixie Highway, about forty miles north of Daytona, when the chauffeur lost control of his vehicle. It turned over and Annie was pinned under the car. She was admitted to Bohannon Hospital, Daytona, where she lay for weeks with a fractured hip and a shattered right ankle. She would never hunt again.

After two years of convalescence in Florida, the couple moved to Dayton, Ohio. Annie's health steadily declined. She was developing anaemia, and was tired and pale. She tried to write her autobiography, but was unable to find the strength to complete it. On 7 October 1925, Annie Oakley Butler wrote her last will and testament. By early 1926, she could only leave her bed for part of the day.

One afternoon in April, Frank brought a surprise visitor, a friend from the UMC days. Will Rogers now wrote a newspaper column read throughout America. A week after his visit, Frank picked up the newspaper and saw Will's column. It was dedicated to Annie, and read:

'This is a good story about a little woman that all the older generation will remember. She was the reigning sensation of America and Europe during the heyday of Buffalo Bill's Wild West Show. She was their star. Her picture was on more billboards than a modern Gloria Swanson. It was Annie Oakley, the greatest woman rifle shot the world has ever produced. Nobody took her place. There was only one. She is bedridden from an automobile accident a few years ago. I want you to write her, all you who remember her, and those that can go and see her. Her address is 706 Lexington Avenue, Dayton, Ohio. She will be a lesson to you. She is a greater character than she was a rifle shot.'

Annie received one thousand letters in the few days after the column appeared. But even a thousand well-wishers could not bring back Annie's health. That summer, she moved back home to Ansonia, Darke County, to live with her niece, Bonnie Blakeley. Frank, too, was ill, and he wanted to go south for the winter, but Annie tired very easily now and she had no desire to go. She told Frank to go alone. To please her, but with a heavy heart, he did so.

At eleven o'clock on Wednesday, 3 November 1926, Annie died. Her death certificate read: 'Annie Oakley Butler. Occupation: Expert marksman. Cause of death: Pernicious anaemia.'

On 4 November it was announced to the world over the Associated Press Wire: 'In the hills of Darke County, Ohio, where the girl, Annie Oakley, learned to handle a rifle, will rest the ashes of the noted marksman, who was perhaps the greatest shooter of all time, the friend of monarchs and the confidante of Sitting Bull.' On the morning of 5 November, a private funeral service was held, and she was cremated the same afternoon in Cincinnati. Her ashes were taken home in an urn to await Frank's death.

It was not a long wait. Frank lay ill in Michigan, where he had been forced to make a prolonged stop on his way to Florida. He died on 21 November

1926, just eighteen days after Annie. The loving couple had been married for forty-two years.

On Thanksgiving Day, 25 November 1926, Annie Oakley and Frank Butler were buried in a little cemetery just a few miles from Annie's childhood home. In the old Brock cemetery, two stones of russet marble, each bearing a simple inscription, stand together:

Annie Oakley	Frank Butler
At Rest	At Rest
1926	1926

While Annie's most devoted fans still make the pilgrimage to the overgrown cemetery in Darke County, millions of others have fallen in love over the years with the little girl from Ohio, immortalized on Broadway stage and silver screen. Sharpshooting Annie and her husband could never have dreamed that Annie would live again. But no doubt they would smile from their graves if they knew that even today, somewhere, in a darkened cinema, those far too young to have ever seen Little Sureshot on stage still hold their breath as she gallops into the ring.